Communicating *with* Friends

communicate better

by Deena Borchers

Group®
Loveland, Colorado

Group®

Communicating With Friends
Copyright © 1992 by Group Publishing, Inc.

Credits
Edited by Michael Warden
Cover designed by Diane Whisner
Interior designed by Judy Bienick and Jan Aufdemberge
Illustrations by Raymond Medici
Photo by David Priest

ISBN 1-55945-228-5
13 12 11 10 9 8 7 6 5 4   03 02 01 00 99 98 97 96 95 94
Printed in the United States of America.

CONTENTS

COMMUNICATING WITH FRIENDS

What's the big deal about communicating clearly? Ask the person who missed an important meeting because the time was misprinted in a memo; the traveler who didn't hear the last call for boarding a flight; or the person who once thought Christians were cannibals because they regularly ate Christ's body and drank his blood!

Miscommunication can lead to problems ranging from doing the wrong homework assignment to international war. And when it comes to understanding and telling others about the Christian faith, the stakes are eternal.

In the church's early history, Christians were often accused of killing children because they immersed them for baptism, or of being cannibals because people didn't understand what was meant by eating "the body of Christ" at Communion.

Today the misunderstandings about Christians and the church are more abstract, but the results are just as saddening. Because of poor communication, the message of Christ is lost, and people's lives are not changed.

We choose many different ways to communicate with each other. We act, gesture, tell a story and use a multitude of other means to get our message across. But communication goes far beyond our surface intentions. Every action, every word, every silence communicates, or sometimes miscommunicates, to those around us. As Christians this means we must be especially careful to think about what our actions will convey to people about Christ and our belief in his redeeming love.

This course helps teenagers take a serious look at how and what they communicate to those around them. It helps them learn how to listen to others, how to resolve conflicts effectively and how to use communication as a tool that reflects their faith in God.

Teenagers *can* learn to communicate effectively. *Communicating With Friends* can give them the understanding they need to begin.

By the end of this course your students will:
- understand the importance of effective communication in all aspects of life, especially those involving faith;
- realize the role of listening in effective communication and practice listening skills;
- discover reasons communication breaks down and methods to minimize the damage when this happens; and
- see examples of both ineffective and effective communication in the Bible.

COURSE OBJECTIVES

HOW TO USE THIS COURSE

ACTIVE LEARNING

Think back on an important lesson you've learned in life. Did you learn it from reading about it? from hearing about it? from something you experienced? Chances are the most important lessons you've learned came from something you've experienced. That's what active learning is—learning by doing. And active learning is a key element in Group's Active Bible Curriculum™.

Active learning leads students in doing things that help them understand important principles, messages and ideas. It's a discovery process that helps kids internalize what they learn.

Each lesson section in Group's Active Bible Curriculum™ plays an important part in active learning:

The **Opener** involves kids in the topic in fun and unusual ways.

The **Action and Reflection** includes an experience designed to evoke specific feelings in the students. This section also processes those feelings through "How did you feel?" questions and applies the message to situations kids face.

The **Bible Application** actively connects the topic with the Bible. It helps kids see how the Bible is relevant to the situations they face.

The **Commitment** helps students internalize the Bible's message and commit to making changes in their lives.

The **Closing** funnels the lesson's message into a time of creative reflection and prayer.

When you put all the sections together, you get a lesson that's fun to teach. And kids get messages they'll remember.

BEFORE THE 4-WEEK SESSION

● Read the Introduction, the Course Objectives and This Course at a Glance.

● Decide how you'll publicize the course using the clip art on the Publicity Page (p. 9). Prepare fliers, newsletter articles and posters as needed.

● Look at the Bonus Ideas (p. 39) and decide which ones you'll use.

● Read the opening statements, Objectives and Bible Basis for the lesson. The Bible Basis shows how specific passages relate to senior highers today.

● Choose which Opener and Closing options to use. Each is appropriate for a different kind of group.

● Gather necessary supplies from This Lesson at a Glance.

● Read each section of the lesson. Adjust where necessary for your class size and meeting room.

BEFORE EACH LESSON

● The approximate minutes listed give you an idea of how long each activity will take. Each lesson is designed to take 35 to 60 minutes. Shorten or lengthen activities as needed to fit your group.

● If you see you're going to have extra time, do an activity or two from the "If You Still Have Time..." box or from the Bonus Ideas (p. 39).

● Dive into the activities with the kids. Don't be a spectator. The lesson will be more successful and rewarding to both you and your students.

● Though some kids may at first think certain activities are "silly," they'll enjoy them, and they'll remember the messages from these activities long after the lesson is over. As one Active Bible Curriculum™ user has said, "I can ask the kids questions about a lesson I did three weeks ago and they actually remember what I taught!" And that's the whole idea of teaching... isn't it?

Have fun with the activities you lead. Remember, it is Jesus who encourages us to become "like little children." Besides, how often do your kids get *permission* to express their childlike qualities?

HELPFUL HINTS

● The answers given after discussion questions are responses your students *might* give. They aren't the only answers or the "right" answers. If needed, use them to spark discussion. Kids won't always say what you wish they'd say. That's why some of the responses given are negative or controversial. If someone responds negatively, don't be shocked. Accept the person, and use the opportunity to explore other angles of the issue.

THIS COURSE AT A GLANCE

Before you dive into the lessons, familiarize yourself with each lesson aim. Then read the scripture passages.
- Study them as a background to the lessons.
- Use them as a basis for your personal devotions.
- Think about how they relate to kids' circumstances today.

LESSON 1: COMMUNICATION: WHAT'S AT STAKE?

Lesson Aim: To help senior highers understand the importance of good communication skills.

Bible Basis: Matthew 15:21-28 and Luke 9:44-45.

LESSON 2: THE LOST ART OF LISTENING

Lesson Aim: To help senior highers discover the vital role listening plays in effective communication.

Bible Basis: Mark 4:24-25 and John 18:33-38.

LESSON 3: WHEN COMMUNICATION BREAKS DOWN

Lesson Aim: To help senior highers discover dangers of ineffective communication and identify methods of avoiding them.

Bible Basis: Matthew 16:5-12 and John 3:1-13.

LESSON 4: HANDLING CONFLICT

Lesson Aim: To help senior highers handle conflict in ways that reflect their faith.

Bible Basis: Luke 4:16-30 and Acts 26:24-31.

PUBLICITY PAGE

Grab your senior highers' attention! Photocopy this page and then cut out and paste the clip art of your choice in your church bulletin or newsletter to advertise this course on communicating. Or photocopy and use the ready-made flier as a bulletin insert. Permission to photocopy this clip art is granted for local church use.

Splash the clip art on posters, fliers or even postcards! Just add the vital details: the date and time the course begins, and where you'll meet.

It's that simple.

Communicating *with* Friends

Communicating *with* Friends

Come to _____

On _____

At _____

Come learn to say what you really mean—and to hear what others have to say at the same time!

A 4-week high school course on communicating more effectively

COMMUNICATING WITH FRIENDS

COMMUNICATION: WHAT'S AT STAKE?

Contrary to the opinions of some, communication isn't optional for humans. Everything we do, say, or fail to say, communicates a message to those around us. If we want to avoid misunderstanding and conflict, and work effectively within our relationships, we need to master effective communication skills.

To help senior highers understand the importance of good communication skills.

LESSON AIM

Students will:
- **recognize some aspects of effective and ineffective communication;**
- **see the benefits of effective communication and the dangers of ineffective communication;**
- **identify ways Jesus communicated effectively; and**
- **discover misunderstandings in communication.**

OBJECTIVES

Look up the following scriptures. Then read the background paragraphs to see how the passages relate to your senior highers.

Matthew 15:21-28 tells the story of a Canaanite woman who wants Jesus to help her daughter.

In their conversation, the woman clearly perceives Jesus' meaning when he likens her people to dogs begging under the table of God's children, Israel. Her understanding and ability to answer this challenge by extending his metaphor wins her

BIBLE BASIS
MATTHEW 15:21-28
LUKE 9:44-45

the help she seeks on behalf of her daughter.

Kids may find this passage startling, since it appears that Jesus is refusing to help someone in need. But a closer look reveals that Jesus was testing the woman's heart to see if her request was sincere. By listening to each other carefully, kids can also learn to see beyond the surface to the real meaning behind people's words.

In **Luke 9:44-45**, Jesus tells his disciples plainly what will happen in the coming days.

Even when Jesus speaks without parables, the disciples can't understand what he's telling them. They're afraid to ask for clarification and fail to comprehend what's happening until after Jesus' death and resurrection.

Like the disciples, teenagers are often fearful when it comes to asking questions. In a world where everyone is supposed to act like they have all the answers, admitting you don't understand something can be quite a stretch. Kids need to learn that it's okay to be confused, but it's not healthy to choose to stay that way.

THIS LESSON AT A GLANCE

Section	Minutes	What Students Will Do	Supplies
Opener (Option 1)	5 to 10	**What Did You Say?**—Follow mumbled instructions.	Pencils, paper
(Option 2)		**What Do We Mean?**—Interpret the meanings of non-verbal cues.	Pencils, paper
Action and Reflection	15 to 20	**Say It Again, Sam**—Reproduce a pattern with only verbal instructions.	"Pattern" handouts (p. 18), paper, pencils, 2 packages of Certs
Bible Application	10 to 15	**Master Methods**—Identify ways Jesus communicated.	Bibles, tape, newsprint, markers
Commitment	5 to 10	**Making It Stick**—Students will choose one way to become better communicators.	3x5 cards, pencils
Closing (Option 1)	up to 5	**Saying What We Mean**—Act out confusing "figures of speech."	Newsprint, marker, tape
(Option 2)		**Being Specific**—Mix a drink from random choices.	Pitchers, milk, water, small containers, powdered drink mixes, cups, spoons

The Lesson

☐ OPTION 1: WHAT DID YOU SAY?

After kids arrive, quietly mumble to the class: **Take a pencil and a sheet of paper from the middle of the floor.**

Pause to let students react by following the instruction or asking for clarification, then mumble: **Write your name at the top of the paper.** Add other instructions in a mumbled voice such as "List your favorite food under your name" or "Draw a picture of your family pet." Kids will probably get frustrated with you and ask for clarification. If they do, repeat the instructions a bit more clearly until kids stop asking for clarification.

When you've given all of the instructions, ask:

● **How did you feel as I gave you mumbled instructions? Explain.** (Frustrated, I couldn't understand you; confused, I couldn't tell what you wanted since you mumbled.)

● **Do you usually ask for clarification when you don't understand someone's request? Why or why not?** (Yes, when I want to know what they said; no, not when I don't care what they want.)

● **What can happen when you don't ask for clarification?** (Nothing gets accomplished; I end up doing something I wasn't asked to do.)

Say: **Today we're going to talk about the role communication plays in our lives, and why it's important to communicate as clearly as we can.**

☐ OPTION 2: WHAT DO WE MEAN?

Give kids pencils and paper. Ask students to number their papers from one to 10, and write the meanings of the following non-verbal messages you convey:

1. Shrug shoulders. ("I don't know.")
2. Point index finger straight up. ("Wait just one moment" or "I'll take one of those" or "We're number one.")
3. Point in a particular direction. ("That way" or "Go away.")
4. Hold arm out with palm up. ("Give me _____" or "Let me help you.")
5. Extend arm with palm facing forward. ("Stop.")
6. Hold out both arms. ("Welcome.")
7. Hold your elbow, with a look of pain. ("My elbow hurts.")
8. Rest head on fist. ("I'm thinking.")
9. Hold hands over ears. ("I don't want to listen.")
10. Tap fingers on the table. ("I'm impatient" or "I'm bored.")

OPENER
(5 to 10 minutes)

When you've finished, have kids tell what they wrote, and point out variations in kids' perceptions.

Ask:

● **What are some other common non-verbal messages?** (A smile or hug; some gestures I can't demonstrate.)

Have volunteers demonstrate non-verbal messages for the whole group to guess.

Then ask:

● **Even though these gestures have fairly universal meanings, do others understand what you're communicating when you use them? Why or why not?** (Yes, usually; no, sometimes they read more into my actions than I intend.)

Say: **Even when we do our best to get a message across, sometimes our communication gets scrambled and misunderstood. Today we're going to talk about the importance of clear communication in our relationships.**

SAY IT AGAIN, SAM

Form pairs and have partners sit back to back. Give one partner in each pair a copy of the "Pattern" handout (p. 18). Give the other partner in each pair a sheet of paper and a pencil. Make sure none of the kids with pencils can see anyone else's handout.

Tell pairs that they are to reproduce the handout on the blank sheet of paper by giving only verbal instructions to the partner with the pencil and paper. The partner who is drawing may ask for clarification. Explain that the pair that creates the best copy of the handout will win a prize.

When pairs are finished, have each show their creation. Have kids vote on which copy best approximates the handout, and give the winning partners each a roll of Certs (or a similar breath freshener).

Ask:

● **Why was this experience difficult?** (I couldn't put what I saw into words; my partner's instructions didn't make sense.)

● **How did you feel when the communication was unclear?** (Frustrated; I wanted to give up.)

● **How are the problems we had in this experience like the problems we have communicating in relationships?** (It's easy to be misunderstood; I get frustrated when people don't really listen to me.)

● **Based on this experience, why is it important to work at communicating clearly?** (I want to be understood; we won't know how to help people if we can't really understand what they're trying to say.)

Say: **Learning to communicate clearly is vital if we want to have successful relationships with others. But communication involves more than simply reproducing a pattern on a page. It involves feelings, hopes and questions, as well as direct thoughts. Let's see how Jesus—the master**

ACTION AND REFLECTION

(15 to 20 minutes)

communicator—dealt with communicating on all these levels.

MASTER METHODS

Form two groups, and assign each group one of these passages: Matthew 15:21-28 or Luke 9:44-45. Tape a sheet of newsprint to the wall and draw a line down the middle. Give kids each a marker. On the newsprint, have groups each list all the methods Jesus used in their passage to communicate with others.

While groups are working, tape another sheet of newsprint to the wall. When groups finish, have them explain what they wrote.

Then ask:

● **Were you surprised by Jesus' methods in these passages? Why or why not?** (Yes, he seemed to be cruel to the woman; no, he was just trying to make his disciples understand what was going to happen.)

● **Besides what you've listed here, what other ways did Jesus communicate?** (He spoke in parables; he communicated God's love by dying on the cross.)

Add kids' responses to their lists. On the second sheet of newsprint, have kids jot down situations where they could appropriately use one or more of Jesus' methods for communicating. When kids are finished, have them each explain what they wrote.

Say: **As we can see, there are lots of good ways to communicate with others. But it takes wisdom to know which method to use in which situation.**

Ask:

● **How do we gain the wisdom we need to communicate effectively?** (Study what Jesus did in the Bible; learn from people we think are good communicators.)

MAKING IT STICK

Give kids 3×5 cards and pencils. From the lists on the wall and from their discussion, have kids each write on their card one way they'll work to become a better communicator at home, school, church or work. Encourage kids to be specific and to make their commitment measurable. For example, "Ask more questions" is a good commitment, while "Listen better" is a little vague.

When kids are finished, have volunteers tell what they wrote. Encourage kids to place their commitments in their Bibles, or tape them to their bedroom mirrors, so they won't lose sight of their goals. Form pairs and have kids each tell their partner one way they think that person is a good communicator. For example, someone might say "You ask questions if you don't understand something" or "You say things clearly so others understand."

BIBLE APPLICATION
(10 to 15 minutes)

COMMITMENT
(5 to 10 minutes)

Table Talk

The Table Talk activity in this course helps senior highers talk with their parents about communicating effectively.

If you choose to use the Table Talk activity, this is a good time to show students the "Table Talk" handout (p. 19). Ask them to spend time with their parents completing it. Tell kids each to be prepared to report on their experience with the handout next week.

Before kids leave, give them each the "Table Talk" handout to take home, or tell them you'll be sending it to their parents.

Or use the Table Talk idea found in the Bonus Ideas (p. 40) for a meeting based on the handout.

CLOSING
(up to 5 minutes)

Say: **All of us have the makings of great communicators. Once we understand our need to communicate clearly, learning to do it is easier.**

☐ OPTION 1: SAYING WHAT WE MEAN

Say: **To close our meeting today, let's take a fun look at ways we can be misunderstood.**

On a sheet of newsprint, write these "figures of speech":

- give me a break
- keep your pants on
- give him a big hand
- knock it off
- the buck stops here
- you look like a million bucks
- chew the fat
- heard it through the grapevine
- break a leg
- drop her a line
- they had me in stitches
- groovy
- hold your horses
- really came through in the clutch

Have volunteers each choose and act out how one of these phrases might be understood by someone from a foreign country. Other students should guess which phrase is being acted out. Say: **It's a good thing people don't always take us literally.**

Close with prayer, thanking God for helping kids to become better communicators.

☐ OPTION 2: BEING SPECIFIC

Before the lesson, prepare two matching, opaque pitchers of liquid (one milk, one water) and two smaller opaque containers of powdered drink mixes (one with instant chocolate milk mix, one with a drink mix such as Tang or Kool-Aid). Provide cups and spoons. Put a barrier between the pitchers and containers and the students.

Say: **Let's close our meeting today by giving everyone a refreshing drink.**

Ask kids, one at a time, to come to the other side of the barrier and mix a "drink" by choosing liquid from a pitcher and powdered drink mix from a small container. Don't give any clues about the contents. When everyone has chosen and mixed, have kids taste their drinks, then discuss the importance of giving complete and accurate instructions.

Say: **From this activity, we can see that often what we don't say can harm us as much as what we do say.**

Close with prayer, asking God to help kids have wisdom to communicate clearly in all their relationships.

If You Still Have Time . . .

Impressions—Form pairs and blindfold one partner in each pair. Have the sighted partner choose several objects to place in his or her partner's hands. Have the blindfolded partners each say what message their partner might be trying to communicate through the objects. For example, giving scissors and paper might mean the blindfolded partner is supposed to cut the paper in two.

According to Mark—Have kids look at Mark's account of Jesus' encounter with the Canaanite woman (Mark 7:24-30). Have kids search for differences in the accounts and discuss why Mark focused on some things Luke chose to ignore and vice versa. Talk about how perceptions of surroundings influence how and what people communicate.

PATTERN

Table Talk

To the Parent: We're involved in a high school course at church called *Communicating With Friends*. Students are exploring a Christian perspective on effective communication. We'd like you and your teenager to spend some time discussing this important topic. Use this "Table Talk" page to help you do that.

Parent

Complete the following sentences:

- One thing my family never talked about when I was young was . . .
- One thing my children talk about that makes me uncomfortable is . . .
- One thing I wish I could do better as a communicator is . . .
- One way I wish communication with my teenager could change is . . .
- The one message I want to get across to my teenager is . . .

Senior higher

Complete the following sentences:

- One thing I really like to talk about is . . .
- What I like most about talking with my parent(s) is . . .
- Concerning communication, it really bothers me when my parent(s) . . .
- One thing I would like to talk to my parent(s) about more often is . . .
- The one message I want to get across to my parent(s) is . . .

Parent and senior higher

Tell how the following statements make you feel. Do you agree or disagree? Explain.

- There are some things that parents just can't understand.
- There are some things that kids just can't understand.
- It's sometimes better not to communicate if talking means we'll get into an argument.
- I let you know when something happens at home that I don't agree with.
- I feel listened to at home, and my opinions are respected.

Together, determine the strengths and weaknesses of your communication at home. Then read Ephesians 4:15-16, and talk about how you can improve communication at home, so that you each encourage the other family members, rather than discourage them.

LESSON 2

THE LOST ART OF LISTENING

Everyone knows what it's like to try to convey an important message and feel that the message isn't being heard. Listening is as much a part of effective communication as talking is—and possibly, even more important. Teenagers, as well as adults, need to know that until we learn to listen, we won't have much of value to say.

LESSON AIM

To help senior highers discover the vital role listening plays in effective communication.

OBJECTIVES

Students will:
- discover distractions that keep people from listening;
- commit to become better listeners;
- study a conversation and instructions on listening from the Bible; and
- practice good listening skills.

BIBLE BASIS
MARK 4:24-25
JOHN 18:33-38

Look up the following scriptures. Then read the background paragraphs to see how the passages relate to your senior highers.

In **Mark 4:24-25**, Jesus warns his disciples to be careful about how they listen.

Often, when Jesus told a parable, he would conclude by saying, "If anyone has ears to hear, let him hear." In this passage, he expounds on what he means by reminding the disciples to be careful not only in what they listen to, but how they listen as well.

Teenagers, especially senior highers, sometimes want to believe they already have all the answers to life. Like Jesus' disciples, kids need to develop listening skills—not only in discerning what they should listen to, but also to pay attention to the *way* they listen.

In **John 18:33-38**, Jesus meets with Pilate before the crucifixion.

In the encounter between Jesus and Pilate, it seems that no effective communication took place. Pilate's focus is political, but Jesus' only concern is the spiritual implications of what he's about to go through. Pilate never sees what Jesus is really saying because he never moves outside his own perspective.

Kids, like all people, each have a specific view of reality. But only when kids learn to step outside their own "world" and see life from another perspective can they ever communicate effectively.

THIS LESSON AT A GLANCE

Section	Minutes	What Students Will Do	Supplies
Opener (Option 1) (Option 2)	5 to 10	**Are You Listening?**—Follow a series of commands while being distracted. **Listening to No One**—Kids tell the leader about their week while he or she ignores them.	
Action and Reflection	15 to 20	**Repeat After Me**—Participate in a discussion where each person must repeat what the previous person said.	Potato
Bible Application	10 to 15	**Missing the Link**—Examine a conversation between Jesus and Pilate.	Bibles, newsprint, markers
Commitment	5 to 10	**Prayer Poster**—Create a poster about listening to hang in their rooms.	Construction paper, markers
Closing (Option 1) (Option 2)	up to 5	**If They Would Listen**—Kids say what they would tell a particular person if they knew he or she would listen. **Listen to the Music**—Sing songs about listening to God and others.	 Group Songbooks

The Lesson

☐ OPTION 1: ARE YOU LISTENING?

Ask for a volunteer. Give the volunteer a series of commands, such as **stand up beside your chair, turn away from the chair, take five steps forward, turn to the right, lift your left arm to the side, take three steps backward.**

Give each command only once. See how well the volunteer

OPENER
(5 to 10 minutes)

follows the commands. Repeat the activity, but this time have another student distract your volunteer by yelling or waving his or her arms.

Ask:

● **How did you feel the second time I gave the instructions?** (Frustrated; stupid.)

● **What things distract us from listening well?** (Other people; other thoughts.)

● **Why is it important to listen well?** (We can't learn unless we listen; we can't get to know people unless we listen to them.)

Say: **Today we're going to discuss the value of listening to others, and we'll discover some ways we can become better listeners.**

☐ OPTION 2: LISTENING TO NO ONE

Gather students together and say: **Before we get started today, I want to hear about how your week has gone. I'd like each of you to tell me one good thing and one bad thing that's happened this week.**

Have kids take turns telling about their week. If you have more than 12 students, form two groups and have an adult sponsor or another teenager lead the second group.

While kids are talking, make it a point *not* to listen. You (and other adult leaders) could fidget with your hair, tie your shoes or occupy yourself with some mundane project, such as cleaning up the room. When kids are finished sharing, ask:

● **How did you feel about telling me (us) about your week?** (Okay; that I wasn't really listened to.)

● **How do you feel when you talk to someone who isn't really listening to you?** (Angry; that I don't matter.)

● **Why is it important to listen to others?** (So they'll know they're important; so they'll listen to me.)

Say: **Today we're going to talk about the importance of listening, and we'll discover ways each of us can become better listeners.**

Table Talk Follow-Up

If you sent the "Table Talk" handout (p. 19) to parents last week, discuss students' reactions to the activity. Ask volunteers to share what they learned from the discussion with their parents.

ACTION AND REFLECTION

(15 to 20 minutes)

REPEAT AFTER ME

Form a circle. Tell students you're going to have a hot-potato discussion about communicating with parents. Ask kids each to think about the thing that's hardest about communicating with parents and the thing that's easiest about it.

Before you begin the discussion, hold up a potato and explain that kids will toss the potato to someone at random to share their response. Also explain that before each person speaks, he or she must restate what the previous person said. This will encourage kids to really listen to others' responses. Toss the potato to someone to start the discussion.

After everyone has shared, ask:

● **How did it feel to listen carefully to the statements of others? Explain.** (Fine, I usually do anyway; weird, I was listening so hard I forgot what I was going to say.)

● **How did it feel to have others listening carefully to your words? Explain.** (Awkward, I was in the spotlight; important, they wanted to hear what I said.)

● **How would school, home or other activities be different if people always listened this way?** (We would understand each other better; we wouldn't argue so much.)

● **What has this experience taught you about being a better listener?** (Listening is fun; I don't need to worry about what *I'm* going to say all the time; it's good to repeat what someone else says so I get it right.)

Say: **Listening leads to greater understanding. It helps avoid fights and lets others know you really care about them.**

MISSING THE LINK

Form two groups—the "Jesus" group and the "Pilate" group. Give each group a Bible, newsprint and a marker. On the top of one sheet, have a student in the Jesus group write "Jesus' Perspective," and on the other, have a student in the Pilate group write "Pilate's Perspective."

Say: **In this passage, Pilate never really understood what Jesus was telling him. I'll assign each group a different perspective to look at.**

Say to the Jesus group: **Read John 18:33-38. Then write the message you think Jesus was trying to convey to Pilate.**

Say to the Pilate group: **Read John 18:33-38. Then write what you think Pilate was hearing Jesus say.**

When groups are ready, have them each tell what they wrote.

Ask:

● **What kept Pilate from really hearing what Jesus was telling him?** (He saw Jesus as a threat to his power; he didn't really understand or ask more about Jesus' perspective.)

● **What sometimes keeps us from really hearing others?** (We've already made up our minds about what they're talking about; we don't really care what they're saying; we're distracted by other things around us.)

Have a volunteer read aloud Mark 4:24-25. Ask:

● **What does this passage tell us about the value of**

BIBLE APPLICATION
(10 to 15 minutes)

listening? (The way I listen to others is likely the way they'll listen to me; a person who listens will gain more understanding; a person who doesn't listen will lose the understanding he or she already has.)

● **What are some things a good listener does?** (Gives you his or her full attention; asks questions.)

● **Based on what we've talked about so far, do you think you are a good listener? Why or why not?** (Yes, I really enjoy getting involved with other people; no, I have a hard time concentrating on what is said.)

● **What are some other things we can do to become better listeners?** (Don't talk as much; make eye contact.)

Say: **With a little effort, and the tips we've discussed today, all of us can learn to be better listeners. Not only will those around us benefit, but we'll be better off too.**

PRAYER POSTER

Form pairs and provide each pair with construction paper and markers. Have kids each create a small poster that says, "Listen." When kids are finished, have them each write a short commitment prayer on the back of their poster, asking God to help them become a better listener.

Have kids each read their prayer to their partner, then write on their partner's poster one way that person shows that he or she is a good listener.

Say: **Take your poster home and place it in a prominent place in your room, so you can remember your commitment to become a better listener.**

☐ OPTION 1: IF THEY WOULD LISTEN

Say: **We've talked today about becoming better listeners. Let's close by taking a quick look at what would change in your life if you knew for certain another person would listen to you.**

Have kids each think of one thing they would say and who they would say it to, if they knew that person would genuinely listen. Tell kids the person can be anyone from the president of the United States to a parent or friend.

Have volunteers share what they would say and who they would say it to.

Note: This closing requires an environment where kids feel accepted and loved. Be sensitive to your students, and offer frequent encouragement as they share.

After everyone has spoken, join hands and close with prayer, asking God to help each person become a better listener.

COMMITMENT
(5 to 10 minutes)

CLOSING
(up to 5 minutes)

☐ OPTION 2: LISTEN TO THE MUSIC

Say: **We've talked today about the value of listening. Let's close our lesson by singing about it.**

Join together in singing familiar songs about listening to God and others. Here are a few suggestions from *The Group Songbook* (Group Books):

"Thy Word"

"Open Our Eyes"

"Here I Am, Lord"

"Hear, Oh Israel"

After the songs, close with prayer, asking God for help to become better listeners—to him and to each other.

If You Still Have Time . . .

Story Time—Have a volunteer tell a story about his or her life. After the story, test kids' listening abilities with questions such as:

- Where did the story take place?
- When did it happen?
- How did the storyteller feel about the situation?
- How did you feel as you heard the story?

What's That You Say?—Form a circle. Whisper this sentence to the person on your right: The ball bearings busted on my Ford pickup's wheels.

Have the person on your right whisper what you said to the next person, and continue until the sentence gets back to you. Repeat aloud what you heard, then the original sentence. Point out that even when we try to listen, we don't always get the message right.

LESSON 3

WHEN COMMUNICATION BREAKS DOWN

Even when people have the best intentions, communication sometimes breaks down. The results are often insignificant, even amusing. But too often communication breakdowns result in hurt feelings and wasted time or energy. Teenagers can learn to deal effectively with problems such as these.

LESSON AIM

To help senior highers discover dangers of ineffective communication and identify methods of avoiding them.

OBJECTIVES

Students will:
● discover more effective communication skills;
● see both comic and destructive results of ineffective communication;
● find ways of minimizing damage when communication breaks down; and
● identify some ways Jesus dealt with communication breakdowns.

BIBLE BASIS
MATTHEW 16:5-12
JOHN 3:1-13

Look up the following scriptures. Then read the background paragraphs to see how the passages relate to your senior highers.

In **Matthew 16:5-12**, Jesus warns his disciples to beware of the leaven of the Pharisees and Saducees.

This passage gives the account of Jesus' almost comical conversation with his disciples about yeast. Jesus is talking about the Pharisee's and the Saducee's teachings, but the disciples think he's talking about bread.

Like the disciples, kids sometimes misunderstand what others are saying by wrongly interpreting what they hear. Kids can learn to listen objectively, so they understand what someone is saying from that person's perspective, rather than their own.

John 3:1-13 details the encounter between Jesus and Nicodemus concerning how to enter God's kingdom.

In his encounter with Jesus, Nicodemus didn't understand how one could hope to be "born again." Only as he asked Jesus to explain further did he begin to see that Jesus wasn't talking about a physical birth, but a spiritual one.

Nicodemus could only imagine one kind of birth and thus could not perceive how one could be born of water and spirit. This passage, as the first, has a strong element of comedy. One can almost imagine Jesus' frustration with people who can't comprehend a new idea.

Fortunately, Nicodemus wasn't afraid to ask questions when he didn't understand Jesus' words. Teenagers, too, need to be encouraged to ask questions when what someone is saying doesn't make sense to them.

THIS LESSON AT A GLANCE

Section	Minutes	What Students Will Do	Supplies
Opener (Option 1)	5 to 10	**Piecing It Together**—Re-create a cut-up Bible verse with limited speaking.	Paper, marker, Bible, scissors
(Option 2)		**Get the Message**—Copy a sentence several times, changing it a little each time.	Paper, pencils
Action and Reflection	15 to 20	**Don't Say It**—Get individuals to act out and guess complicated actions without speaking to them.	
Bible Application	10 to 15	**Do You Hear What I Mean?**—Explore how Jesus handled breakdowns in communication.	Bibles
Commitment	5 to 10	**Communication Diary**—Agree to keep a diary of communication for one week.	Paper, pens
Closing (Option 1)	up to 5	**Unbroken**—Compare the activity of holding hands and leaning back to communication.	
(Option 2)		**Comic Breakup**—Create a comic strip based on a personal experience of a communication breakdown.	Paper, pencils

THE LESSON

☐ OPTION 1: PIECING IT TOGETHER

Using a large sheet of paper and a marker, copy 1 Thessalonians 5:11 in large letters and cut it into single words.

As kids arrive, give kids each a word and tell them not to discuss it yet. It's okay if more than one person is assigned to the same word or if one person has more than one word.

Say: **Each of you holds part of a verse in 1 Thessalonians. You must work together to re-create the verse. But the only word you may speak is the one you are holding. Go!**

After a few minutes, or when kids think they've found the answer, read the verse from the Bible. Ask:

● **What was hard about this game?** (We could only say one word so we didn't understand each other well; we weren't familiar with the verse.)

● **In this activity, how did communication break down?** (I couldn't get across what I was trying to say; we couldn't agree on how to arrange the words.)

Say: **Communication can break down in even the best of circumstances. Today we're going to discuss how to handle this often volatile situation.**

☐ OPTION 2: GET THE MESSAGE

Form a circle. If you have more than 10 kids, form two or more circles. Give kids each a slip of paper and a pencil. On your own slip of paper, write a sentence such as, "It's becoming clear to me now that I'm not sounding clear to you." Pass the slip to your right. Have that person copy your sentence, replacing one word of his or her choosing with a new word. Then have that person pass his or her slip to the next person. Continue having kids copy the sentence, changing one word, until it gets back to you.

Compare the original sentence to the sentence you ended up with.

Ask:

● **How did communication break down in this experiment?** (We each made a small change in what we read before passing it on; we relied on what the person next to us wrote, rather than going to the source.)

Say: **Today we're going to talk about how communication breaks down in real life and what we can do about it.**

DON'T SAY IT

Form groups of five or fewer. Have each group designate one person to act as the "Receiver." Send all the Receivers out of the room.

While the Receivers are gone, have groups each come up with three to five "actions" they'll get the Receiver to act out with them—without talking. Tell groups to make the actions wild and crazy, but identifiable. Explain that groups will have to get their Receivers to guess what actions they are acting out with their other group members.

Offer suggestions to get groups thinking on the right track; for example, eating a bologna sandwich while riding on the wing of an airplane; or watching Indiana Jones movies while resting on the bottom of the ocean.

Tell kids they can use their arms and legs, and make any noise they want—even hum a tune—as long as they don't *say* any words. When groups are ready, call all the Receivers and explain to them what's expected of them. Allow groups to go one at a time, congratulating Receivers if they guess correctly.

After all the groups have had their fun, ask:

● **What made this game so much fun?** (Having people act out and guess goofy things; trying to communicate something very original without words.)

● **How did you feel as you tried to get your message across to your Receiver?** (Frustrated, I couldn't get the message across; frustrated, the Receiver couldn't understand what my actions meant.)

● **How did you feel as a Receiver?** (Angry, they didn't act it out well enough that I could guess it; stupid, I couldn't understand what they were trying to get me to do.)

● **How is this experience like or unlike communication breakdown in real life? Explain.** (Unlike real life, it usually isn't this funny; like real life, you feel frustrated because you're not being understood.)

● **What should we do when communication breaks down in real life?** (Listen more carefully; talk it out as soon as possible.)

Say: **In this game, misunderstandings created a lot of fun. But in real life, misunderstandings can lead to tough problems and wasted energy. Let's see how Jesus handled some of the misunderstandings he faced.**

DO YOU HEAR WHAT I MEAN?

Form two groups and assign each group one of these passages to present as a skit: Matthew 16:5-12 or John 3:1-7. Have groups each create their skit and present it to the other group. Then ask each group:

● **What was the misunderstanding in your passage?** (The disciples didn't understand Jesus was talking about the Pharisees' and the Saducees' teachings, not about bread; Nicodemus thought Jesus was telling him he had to go back to his mother's womb in order to get to heaven.)

● **What negative results could have come from this communication breakdown?** (The disciples wouldn't have understood Jesus' warning about the Pharisees and Saducees; Nicodemus wouldn't have understood how to enter God's kingdom.)

● **How did Jesus prevent those negative results from happening?** (He told the disciples they had misunderstood him; he further explained to Nicodemus what he meant by "born again.")

● **What lessons can we learn from Jesus about handling communication breakdowns?** (Question others when you think they're misunderstanding you; be sensitive to what other people are hearing, not just what you're saying.)

Say: **There are lots of good ways to avoid a communication breakdown—saying what you mean in more than one way, asking questions, even asking the other person to repeat what you said. But when communication breakdowns do happen, we should deal with them as soon as possible. That way we can avoid problems for ourselves and others.**

COMMUNICATION DIARY

Give kids each four sheets of paper and a pen. Have kids each fold their papers in half to form a booklet, then put their name on it and title it "Communication Diary."

Say: **To help us learn about communication in our lives, and especially how we deal with communication breakdowns, I'd like for you to commit to keeping a diary for one week. Each day, write a summary of the communication that happened in your relationships that day. Focus on any communication breakdowns that occur and how you handle them.**

As a fun way to get everyone started in this project, have kids pass their diaries around, and have students "communicate" words of encouragement to each other by writing positive things in each other's diaries.

Encourage kids to go back through their diaries at the end of the week and to see what they can do to improve how they handle communication breakdowns.

☐ OPTION 1: UNBROKEN

Form a circle. Say: **Let's pretend our joined hands represent clear communication between each of us in the group.** Join hands and have kids lean backwards.

Ask:

● **What would have happened if I had let go of the person's hand next to me?** (We all would've fallen.)

● **What happens in a group when communication breaks**

COMMITMENT
(5 to 10 minutes)

CLOSING
(up to 5 minutes)

down between two people? (Everyone is affected; we might take sides.)

Say: **When communication breaks down between two people, it has an impact on the whole group. Let's work together to "keep the circle unbroken."**

Close with prayer, asking God to help your youth group learn to deal effectively with communication breakdowns.

☐ OPTION 2: COMIC BREAKUP

Form pairs. Give pairs each a sheet of paper and a pencil to create a comic strip based on an experience of a communication breakdown. When everyone is finished, have pairs explain their comic strips.

Say: **It can be easy to make jokes about misunderstandings in our relationships, but it's important to remember always to handle communication breakdowns with sensitivity and love.**

Close with prayer, asking God to help kids learn to handle the communication breakdowns in their lives in ways that are pleasing to God.

If You Still Have Time . . .

Discovering Prejudice—Ask the students to pretend they are police officers listening to the testimony of a person who has been mugged. Tell them to envision the crime as they hear it reported.

Read this report: **I was walking down Maple Street when a person came up to me from behind and demanded my valuables. I could feel a small hard object pressed against my back, so I just handed my rings and watch back without looking. I was really scared.**

The person took my things, pushed me down so that I fell hard on the sidewalk, then ran. I let the sound of the running feet get really far away before I got up to go find help.

After the reading, ask students to honestly answer these questions based on the scene they envisioned: **Did this crime take place in a city or small town? Was the victim male or female? Was the victim young or old? How was the victim dressed? Was the assailant male or female? Was the assailant young or old? What did the assailant threaten the victim with? What was the assailant's motive?**

After asking the questions, discuss how our stereotypes can affect clear communication with others.

Name That Message—Play a variation of "Name That Tune," except have kids try to guess simple commands giving the fewest words possible, instead of giving musical notes. Here are some possible commands you can use:

- no smoking in the auditorium;
- stay off the grass;
- no shirt, no shoes, no service;
- no right turn on red;
- clean your room;
- do your homework;
- right lane must turn right.

LESSON 4

HANDLING CONFLICT

We all have been in the uncomfortable position of dealing with a conflict caused by ineffective communication. The ability to deal in a healthy and constructive way with such conflict is an important skill we'll use throughout our lives.

LESSON AIM

To help senior highers handle conflict in ways that reflect their faith.

OBJECTIVES

Students will:
- **examine ways conflict is handled in the Bible;**
- **experience disagreement caused by ineffective communication;**
- **discuss problems in communication which can lead to conflict; and**
- **learn ways to avoid misunderstanding and conflict.**

BIBLE BASIS
LUKE 4:16-30
ACTS 26:24-31

Look up the following scriptures. Then read the background paragraphs to see how the passages relate to your senior highers.

In **Luke 4:16-30**, Jesus confronts the Jews on their lack of belief.

This is one of only a few passages where Jesus gets into physical danger because of what he says. After confronting the Jews, they prepare to throw him off a cliff. Jesus says nothing more, but slips away alone.

Jesus certainly wasn't afraid of a fight. But he had wisdom to know when fighting was unproductive—and even dangerous. Teenagers can gain Christ's insight to know when to stand up to others and when to walk away.

In **Acts 26:24-31**, Paul talks to King Agrippa about the gospel.

This passage gives us a glimpse of Paul's keen way with language. He shows great skill in communicating not only in his own defense, but as a witness for Christ. He's polite, persuasive and relaxed enough to joke with them about his chains. Paul knew when conflict was good and necessary in spreading the gospel and when it wasn't.

Kids can learn from Paul's example ways to deal with aggressive personalities around them. Kids can learn, as Paul did, that often a kind word and a joke hold far more power than an angry roar.

THIS LESSON AT A GLANCE

Section	Minutes	What Students Will Do	Supplies
Opener (Option 1)	5 to 10	**Carbonated Challenge**—Get a drink if they say the right words.	Glasses, chilled soft drink
(Option 2)		**House of Cards**—Try to build a house of cards with each group member following different instructions.	Card decks or 3×5 cards
Action and Reflection	15 to 20	**Hand-to-Hand Combat**—Try to knock their partner off-balance using only the palms of their hands.	
Bible Application	10 to 15	**Dramatize the Crime**—Act out two conflicts from the Bible.	Bibles
Commitment	5 to 10	**Choose to Diffuse**—Make a fist full of reminders for ways to deal effectively with conflict.	Tape, newsprint, marker, 3×5 cards, pencils, scissors, Bible
Closing (Option 1)	up to 5	**Unity**—Read Psalm 133 in unison.	Bibles
(Option 2)		**Cinnamon Roll Hug**—Roll themselves up for a giant hug.	

The Lesson

☐ OPTION 1: CARBONATED CHALLENGE

Distribute glasses as kids arrive. Bring a chilled, unmarked bottle of Pepsi or Coke, and hold it up as you offer to serve it to the kids. As you come to each person, ask:

● **What do you want?**

If kids say anything other than "carbonated liquid," tell them that's the wrong answer and move on to the next person.

OPENER
(5 to 10 minutes)

Go through the group multiple times so kids have a chance to figure out the "correct" answer.

Ask:

● **How did you feel when I didn't give you a drink?** (Frustrated; angry.)

● **What is the conflict that arose from this activity?** (We didn't know the words to say; you wouldn't tell us what you wanted.)

● **How is this conflict like what happens when day-to-day communication isn't clear or is intentionally poor?** (When people aren't clear about things, they feel frustrated or angry; fights start when people aren't communicating well.)

Say: **Today we're going to talk about conflict in communication, and how we can effectively diffuse relationship battles that come from ineffective communication.**

Serve the soft drink to students.

☐ OPTION 2: HOUSE OF CARDS

Form groups of four and give each group a deck of cards or a supply of about 40 3×5 cards. Tell groups to build card towers from their decks. Before they begin, have kids in each group count off from one to four. Call the "ones" together and give them the following secret instruction:

● **Build a tall tower.**

Call the "twos" and give them the following secret instruction:

● **Build a tower not more than one story high.**

Call the "threes" and give them the following secret instruction:

● **Use only face cards to build a tower** (or, if you use 3×5 cards: **Use only cards that are folded in half to build a tower**).

Call the "fours" and give them the following secret instruction:

● **Disagree with everyone's choices on how to build a tower.**

Have groups begin building their towers.

After a few minutes, call groups together and ask:

● **How did you feel as you worked on the card house together? Explain.** (Frustrated, we couldn't work as a team; angry, we couldn't agree.)

● **How is this exercise similar to conflict in real life?** (People want their own way; everyone wants to be in charge.)

● **What did you discover about your group members?** (They had different instructions; they were unwilling to change.)

Note: During this activity, some kids might choose to give in to the rest of the group and follow someone else's instructions. Observe the groups closely to see if this happens. If so, use this opportunity to talk about how sometimes conflict is avoided when people compromise or when people give in to others' ideas. Discuss the positive and negative aspects of compromising or giving in.

Say: **Today we're going to talk about conflict in communication and discover ways we can effectively diffuse the relationship battles that come from ineffective communication.**

HAND-TO-HAND COMBAT

Form pairs and have partners stand about 6 inches apart with their feet spread and their hands shoulder high, palms forward. Tell kids that the goal of this "experiment" is to knock their partners off-balance without losing their own balance in the process. Tell kids they can touch only their partner's hands. Their hands must remain open—no gripping—and their feet must remain on the floor.

Allow kids to do the experiment for several minutes. Every few minutes, tell kids to switch partners and start again.

After several minutes, ask:

● **How did you feel during this experiment? Explain.** (Confident, it was fun; frustrated, my partner pushed too hard.)

● **How is this experiment similar to conflict in your personal life?** (I wanted control of the situation; I fought to get the upper hand.)

● **If slapping each other's hands represents conflict, what physical actions might represent ways to deal effectively with conflict?** (Hugging each other; shaking hands.)

● **What are effective ways to handle real-life conflict that's caused by ineffective communication?** (Talk as soon as possible, but not while you're angry; listen to the other person rather than fighting for your own position.)

● **What are examples of wrong ways to handle conflict caused by ineffective communication?** (Talk about the other person behind his or her back; stop talking to that person.)

Say: **Conflicts don't always have to be like the game we just played. Rather than going head to head or hand to hand against someone, we can make choices that can diffuse even the most volatile situations. We've already talked about several good things we can do. Now let's look at a few more.**

ACTION AND REFLECTION
(15 to 20 minutes)

DRAMATIZE THE CRIME

Form groups of four and assign each group one of these two passages: Luke 4:16-30 or Acts 26:24-31. It's okay if more than one group has the same Bible passage. Tell each group they have seven minutes to create a dramatization of their passage, putting special emphasis on the conflict described there.

After seven minutes, have groups each present their dramatization. Applaud each group's efforts.

Then ask:

● **How would you have handled these situations?** (I would have yelled at Festus; I would have run away.)

● **How did Paul and Jesus deal with the conflicts they faced?** (Jesus left; Paul answered with kindness and humor.)

● **What other effective ways might Jesus and Paul have used?** (There was no other way for Jesus to deal with the situation; Paul could have ignored Festus and just continued talking to Agrippa.)

Say: **Conflict is not fun, but we can actually turn conflict around for good by applying the tips we've discussed today in handling volatile situations.**

CHOOSE TO DIFFUSE

Tape a sheet of newsprint to the wall. Ask kids to brainstorm good, practical ways of dealing with conflict in relationships. If necessary, remind them of ways you've already talked about in the lesson. List these on the newsprint.

Give kids 3×5 cards, pencils and scissors. Have kids each cut their 3×5 card into the shape of a fist. On their fist, tell them each to write one or two tips for dealing with conflict that he or she will start putting into practice this week. Have kids refer to the lists on the newsprint. Tell kids to tape their "fists" to their bedroom mirrors as reminders of their commitments.

Form groups of three and have kids each write on the back of one another's fist one way that person handles conflict well.

Read 1 John 4:7 and say: **By letting Christ's love rule our hearts, we can learn to handle conflict with gentleness and love.**

☐ OPTION 1: UNITY

Form a circle and give everyone a Bible. Have kids read Psalm 133 in unison.

After the psalm, say: **Let's strive to live in unity, not just with each other here, but in all our relationships.**

Close with prayer, thanking God for giving kids the tools to deal effectively with conflicts in relationships.

☐ OPTION 2: CINNAMON ROLL HUG

Tell kids to form a line and join hands. Starting at one end, "roll" the kids up into a giant "cinnamon roll" hug (spiral shape).

Say: **By dealing effectively with conflict, we can be free to enjoy each other's love.**

On the count of three, have everyone "squeeze" in a giant hug, being careful not to hurt those inside the roll.

If You Still Have Time . . .

Communication Diary—Let students discuss the diaries they kept for the previous week's commitment activity. Be sure to praise kids for situations well-handled and encourage those who had difficulty.

Course Reflection—Form a circle. Ask students to reflect on the past four lessons. Have them take turns completing the following sentences:

- Something I learned in this course was . . .
- If I could tell my friends about this course, I'd say . . .
- Something I'll do differently because of this course is . . .

BONUS IDEAS

Bonus Scriptures—The lessons focus on a select few scripture passages, but if you'd like to incorporate more Bible readings into the lesson, here are our suggestions:

- Genesis 27:1-37 (Jacob deceived his father so he could receive the elder son's blessing.)
- Numbers 20:1-13 (Moses didn't heed God's command, and was forbidden entrance into the Promised Land.)
- Proverbs 12:15 (The author compares the listening habits of wise and of foolish people.)
- Matthew 13:11-17 (Jesus explains why he teaches in parables.)
- James 1:19-20 (James admonishes his readers to be quick to listen.)
- James 3:5-12 (James compares the tongue to fire and to a ship's rudder.)

Youth Scoop—To improve the youth group's communication with the church, have kids make plans to start a youth group newsletter. Or ask for a special section in the church's newsletter to print a schedule of youth group activities.

Have kids use the clip art on page 42 as a starting place for ideas in creating their newsletter.

Get the Message—Prepare slips of paper with commands, such as make a sandwich, pour a glass of water, do sit ups, and so on. Also include several slips of paper that say, "I love you." Have kids each draw one slip of paper out of a hat.

Form pairs and have partners each communicate their instruction to their partner without speaking or using props. They can make noises or guide the other person's arms and hands. Kids will know they have adequately communicated their messages when their partners say it to them.

After pairs are finished, discuss the clarity of their directions.

Who's on First?—Get a copy of the Abbot & Costello classic, "Who's on First" and listen to the comic breakdown of communication. Have kids discuss how this comic situation is like and unlike communication breakdowns in real life. For added fun, have volunteers learn the skit and perform it for the whole group.

Media Blitz—Set up a throbbing electronic environment—two or three VCRs playing favorite movies, tape decks with headphones, video games, a table loaded with current popular magazines and newspapers, and an all-news radio or TV

MEETINGS AND MORE

station blaring in one corner. Provide popcorn and turn kids loose in the room for one hour. When one hour has passed, cut the power, gather kids together and read aloud Psalm 46:8-11. Have kids listen to God for five minutes, then talk about what they've learned from the experience.

This Call's for You—Gather kids in a church office or business with two or three open phone lines you can use. Talk about the importance of encouraging each other through communication. Brainstorm a list of church workers, teachers and volunteers in the community. Have kids take turns phoning them and thanking them for what they do in your city. For fun, have pizza delivered. Overwhelm the delivery person with your thanks and appreciation.

Wait for the Beep—Form groups of four or fewer. Give groups each a tape recorder with a blank tape and send them each to a different room. Give groups 15 minutes to create and record the world's best answering machine message. Serve snacks during the "playback" time. Talk about what people learn about us from our planned messages and our unplanned ones.

Table Talk—Use the Table Talk handout (p. 19) as the basis for a meeting with parents and teenagers. During the meeting, have parents and kids complete the handout and discuss it.

Invite kids and parents to share a sit-down meal where they have to express their desires without talking. Follow the meal with charades or Pictionary. Close out the evening with a discussion of the non-verbal messages we give. Include time for parents and teenagers to talk about the communication issues they face in their homes.

PARTY PLEASER

Read my Recipe—Hold a dinner for parents and kids. Provide kids each with a recipe for creating a part of the meal. Have kids sit at tables and give verbal instructions to their parents. Then have parents go to the kitchen and follow the verbal instructions without looking at the recipe themselves. Stress the importance of clarity to parents and kids. Have parents serve the meal when it is ready, and join in for a fun time!

Note: Make sure kids don't tell parents exactly what they're making. Just have them each give instructions in the order they're to be performed.

Bridging the Generation Gap—Invite kids, parents and grandparents (if possible) to spend a weekend together to discuss ways communication has changed over the years. Refer to the "Table Talk" handout (p. 19) for ideas about common problems in communication and how they can be overcome. Have parents and grandparents list ways communication in society has changed *and* stayed the same in the last 30 to 50 years. Discuss how these changes affect the perceptions of each generation and how kids and parents can learn from each other to communicate more effectively.

RETREAT IDEA

CLIP ART IDEAS FOR YOUTH GROUP NEWSLETTER

CURRICULUM REORDER—TOP PRIORITY

Order now to prepare for your upcoming Sunday school classes, youth ministry meetings, and weekend retreats! Each book includes all teacher and student materials—plus photocopiable handouts—for any size class . . . for just $8.99 each!

FOR SENIOR HIGH:

1 & 2 Corinthians: Christian Discipleship, ISBN 1-55945-230-7

Angels, Demons, Miracles & Prayer, ISBN 1-55945-235-8

Changing the World, ISBN 1-55945-236-6

Christians in a Non-Christian World, ISBN 1-55945-224-2

Christlike Leadership, ISBN 1-55945-231-5

Communicating With Friends, ISBN 1-55945-228-5

Counterfeit Religions, ISBN 1-55945-207-2

Dating Decisions, ISBN 1-55945-215-3

Dealing With Life's Pressures, ISBN 1-55945-232-3

Deciphering Jesus' Parables, ISBN 1-55945-237-4

Exodus: Following God, ISBN 1-55945-226-9

Exploring Ethical Issues, ISBN 1-55945-225-0

Faith for Tough Times, ISBN 1-55945-216-1

Forgiveness, ISBN 1-55945-223-4

Getting Along With Parents, ISBN 1-55945-202-1

Getting Along With Your Family, ISBN 1-55945-233-1

The Gospel of John: Jesus' Teachings, ISBN 1-55945-208-0

Hazardous to Your Health: AIDS, Steroids & Eating Disorders, ISBN 1-55945-200-5

Is Marriage in Your Future?, ISBN 1-55945-203-X

Jesus' Death & Resurrection, ISBN 1-55945-211-0

The Joy of Serving, ISBN 1-55945-210-2

Knowing God's Will, ISBN 1-55945-205-6

Life After High School, ISBN 1-55945-220-X

Making Good Decisions, ISBN 1-55945-209-9

Money: A Christian Perspective, ISBN 1-55945-212-9

Movies, Music, TV & Me, ISBN 1-55945-213-7

Overcoming Insecurities, ISBN 1-55945-221-8

Psalms, ISBN 1-55945-234-X

Real People, Real Faith: Amy Grant, Joni Eareckson Tada, Dave Dravecky, Terry Anderson, ISBN 1-55945-238-2

Responding to Injustice, ISBN 1-55945-214-5

Revelation, ISBN 1-55945-229-3

School Struggles, ISBN 1-55945-201-3

Sex: A Christian Perspective, ISBN 1-55945-206-4

Today's Lessons From Yesterday's Prophets, ISBN 1-55945-227-7

Turning Depression Upside Down, ISBN 1-55945-135-1

What Is the Church?, ISBN 1-55945-222-6

Who Is God?, ISBN 1-55945-218-8

Who Is Jesus?, ISBN 1-55945-219-6

Who Is the Holy Spirit?, ISBN 1-55945-217-X

Your Life as a Disciple, ISBN 1-55945-204-8

FOR JUNIOR HIGH/MIDDLE SCHOOL:

Accepting Others: Beyond Barriers & Stereotypes, ISBN 1-55945-126-2

Advice to Young Christians: Exploring Paul's Letters, ISBN 1-55945-146-7

Applying the Bible to Life, ISBN 1-55945-116-5

Becoming Responsible, ISBN 1-55945-109-2

Bible Heroes: Joseph, Esther, Mary & Peter, ISBN 1-55945-137-8

Boosting Self-Esteem, ISBN 1-55945-100-9

Building Better Friendships, ISBN 1-55945-138-6

Can Christians Have Fun?, ISBN 1-55945-134-3

Caring for God's Creation, ISBN 1-55945-121-1

Christmas: A Fresh Look, ISBN 1-55945-124-6

Competition, ISBN 1-55945-133-5

Dealing With Death, ISBN 1-55945-112-2

Dealing With Disappointment, ISBN 1-55945-139-4

Doing Your Best, ISBN 1-55945-142-4

Drugs & Drinking, ISBN 1-55945-118-1

Evil and the Occult, ISBN 1-55945-102-5

Genesis: The Beginnings, ISBN 1-55945-111-4

Guys & Girls: Understanding Each Other, ISBN 1-55945-110-6

Handling Conflict, ISBN 1-55945-125-4

Heaven & Hell, ISBN 1-55945-131-9

Is God Unfair?, ISBN 1-55945-108-4

Love or Infatuation?, ISBN 1-55945-128-9

Making Parents Proud, ISBN 1-55945-107-6

Making the Most of School, ISBN 1-55945-113-0

Materialism, ISBN 1-55945-130-0

The Miracle of Easter, ISBN 1-55945-143-2

Miracles!, ISBN 1-55945-117-3

Peace & War, ISBN 1-55945-123-8

Peer Pressure, ISBN 1-55945-103-3

Prayer, ISBN 1-55945-104-1

Reaching Out to a Hurting World, ISBN 1-55945-140-8

Sermon on the Mount, ISBN 1-55945-129-7

Suicide: The Silent Epidemic, ISBN 1-55945-145-9

Telling Your Friends About Christ, ISBN 1-55945-114-9

The Ten Commandments, ISBN 1-55945-127-0

Today's Faith Heroes: Madeline Manning Mims, Michael W. Smith, Mother Teresa, Bruce Olson, ISBN 1-55945-141-6

Today's Media: Choosing Wisely, ISBN 1-55945-144-0

Today's Music: Good or Bad?, ISBN 1-55945-101-7

What Is God's Purpose for Me?, ISBN 1-55945-132-7

What's a Christian?, ISBN 1-55945-105-X

Order today from your local Christian bookstore, or write: Group Publishing, Box 485, Loveland, CO 80539. For mail orders, please add postage/handling of $4 for orders up to $15, $5 for orders of $15.01+. Colorado residents add 3% sales tax.

MORE PROGRAMMING IDEAS FOR YOUR ACTIVE GROUP...

DO IT! ACTIVE LEARNING IN YOUTH MINISTRY

Thom and Joani Schultz

Discover the keys to teaching creative faith-building lessons that teenagers look forward to...and remember for a lifetime. You'll learn how to design simple, fun programs that will help your kids...

- build community,
- develop communication skills,
- relate better to others,
- experience what it's really like to be a Christian,

...and apply the Bible to their daily challenges. Plus, you'll get 24 ready-to-use active-learning exercises complete with debriefing questions and Bible application. For example, your kids will...

- learn the importance of teamwork and the value of each team member by juggling six different objects as a group,
- experience community and God's grace using a doughnut,
- grow more sensitive to others' needs by acting out Matthew 25:31-46

...just to name a few. And the practical index of over 30 active-learning resources will make your planning easier.

ISBN 0-931529-94-8

DEVOTIONS FOR YOUTH GROUPS ON THE GO

Dan and Cindy Hansen

Now it's easy to turn every youth group trip into an opportunity for spiritual growth for your kids. This resource gives you 52 easy-to-prepare devotions that teach meaningful spiritual lessons using the experiences of your group's favorite outings. You'll get devotions perfect for everything from amusement parks, to choir trips, to miniature golf, to the zoo. Your kids will gain new insights from the Bible as they...

- discuss how many "strikes" God gives us—after enjoying a game of softball,
- experience the hardship of Jesus' temptation in the wilderness—on a camping trip,
- understand the disciples' relief when Jesus calmed the storm—while white-water rafting, even

...learn to trust God's will when bad weather cancels an event or the bus breaks down!

Plus, the handy topical listing makes your planning easy.

ISBN 1-55945-075-4